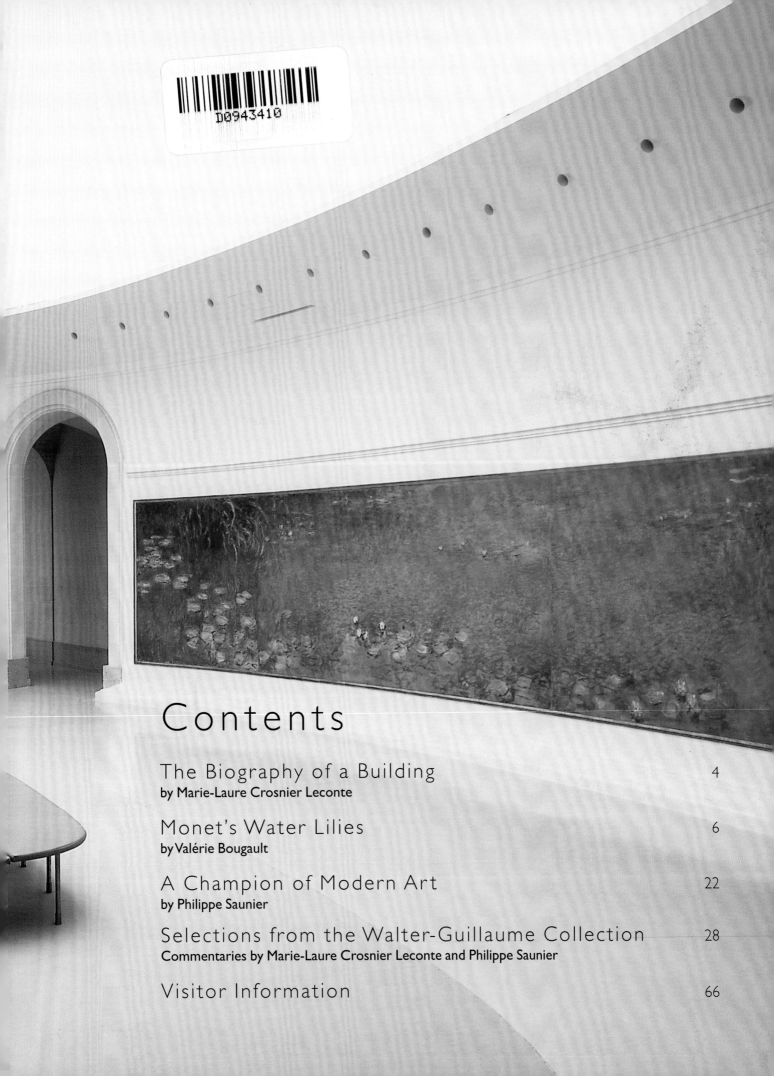

Contents

The Biography of a Building

BY MARIE-LAURE CROSNIER LECONTE

The entrance to the Musée de l'Orangerie in the Tuileries Gardens.

The Renoir and Cézanne gallery in the Walter-Guillaume Collection

View of the Derain and Soutine galleries

At the request of Napoleon III, the Orangerie was built in 1853 by the head architect of the Tuileries, Firmin Bourgeois, as a winter home for the gardens' more fragile plants. As of 1873 it was used for everything from dog shows to entrance exams for the *grandes écoles*. Then, in 1921, it was attributed to the national museums organisation, along with its sister building, the Jeu de Paume, built in 1862 beside the Rue de Rivoli. In 1927 the architect Camille Lefèvre laid out two rooms to house the *Water Lilies* series that Claude Monet had donated to the State in 1922. These were inaugurated in 1927, while the western end of the building was used for temporary exhibitions. Among the hundred or so major shows put on there were 'Painters of Reality in 17th-Century France', in 1934, and, in 1946, an ensemble of masterpieces from French private collec-

tions repatriated from Germany by the Allies. The Orangerie's celebration of Monet on the twenty-fifth anniversary of the painter's death attracted unprecedented numbers of visitors to see the *Water Lilies*. Like the Petit Palais, the gallery became a venue for prestige exhibitions, many of them featuring the Impressionists.

In 1960 the building was transformed in order to house the collection assembled by the art dealer Paul Guillaume, and continued by his widow, Domenica, who went on to marry the architect and businessman Jean Walter. Since Madame Walter wanted these 145 works to be presented in a setting that evoked a domestic interior, the architect Olivier Lahalle created an upper floor running all along the building, with an entrance hall at the west end (decorated by Jansen), followed by a monumental circular staircase with a double

flight of stairs and a handrail by Raymond Subes. To support this, he capped the *Water Lilies* room with a slab of concrete. The Walter-Guillaume Collection was revealed to the public during the first half of 1966, after which Madame Walter took back the paintings that she had promised to the State, but with usufruct.

The Orangerie now resumed its series of major exhibitions, held in the first-floor rooms vacated by the Walter-Guillaume Collection. This cycle, which extended to artists of the twentieth century, reached a distinguished conclusion in 1978 with the presentation of the Pierre and Denise Lévy Donation (held by the modern art museum in Troyes since 1982).

When Domenica Walter died, in 1977, plans could be made for the permanent installation of her collection. The Musée de l'Orangerie reopened in 1984. However, the use of the western end of the ground floor for offices meant there was no space for temporary exhibitions and, even more seriously, cut off access to the *Water Lilies* from the Seine. Visitors now had to take a complicated route in order to reach them. Ten years later, the Orangerie was included in plans to modernise the Louvre and Tuileries. The idea was to restore the coherence of its two permanent ensembles, and to add a room for temporary exhibitions as well as a small auditorium and a resources centre. An architectural competition was held in 1998 and won by the Bordeaux-based firm of Brochet-Lajus-Pueyo. Their design has restored the natural lighting of the *Water Lilies* by recreating their original setting. The upper floor has been demolished and new underground spaces have been built specially to house the Walter-Guillaume Collection. ■

Monet's Water Lilies

Starting in 1893, Claude Monet devoted the last thirty years of his life to an undertaking that was as radical as it was poetic. Inspired by the daily spectacle of the garden at his home in Giverny, his paintings of *Water Lilies* at the Musée de l'Orangerie offer a truly unique visual experience.

BY VALÉRIE BOUGAULT

Claude Monet painting *The Water Lilies* on the day of his 80th birthday in his studio at Giverny.

Green Reflections (detail of the left panel), 1914-18, oil on canvas, 197 x 847 cm.

'Was present: Monsieur Claude Monet, painter, living in Giverny. Who, by the present document, makes an irrevocable *inter vivos* donation to the French State of unrestricted ownership of the works by himself listed hereinafter forming an ensemble of nineteen decorative panels entitled "Water Lilies Series", namely:' There then follows a list of ten compositions, panel by panel, plus this clause: 'The works thus donated shall be destined exclusively to constitute in the Orangerie building in the Tuileries a Claude Monet Museum, comprising two rooms dedicated to the panels listed above with the addition of no other work of painting or sculpture.'

Of course, notarial documents rarely match the lyrical flights of a Péguy or the subtle poetry of Proustian descriptions, and yet it would not be taking a very great risk to suggest that the office of Mâitre Baudrez, a

notary in Vernon, in the department of Eure, was, on 12 April 1922, the theatre of an emotion as powerful as any inspired by great literature. For the greatest living French painter, the last survivor of the Impressionist movement, was bequeathing to his fellow countrymen his great work, with the unusual title of *Nymphéas: Water Lilies*.

This was very nearly the final chapter in a singular artistic adventure that began thirty years earlier. In 1922 Monet was well into the autumn of his life (he died on 5 December 1926), but not at the end of his art.

Having withdrawn to Giverny, on the banks of the Seine, he worked tirelessly on a series of paintings that are without parallel in the history of painting. These went by the titles of 'Pools with Water Lilies' (*Bassins aux nymphéas*, 1895-1900), 'Series of Water Landscapes' (*Paysages d'eau*, 1903–08), 'Japanese Bridges' (*Ponts japonais*, 1914–19),

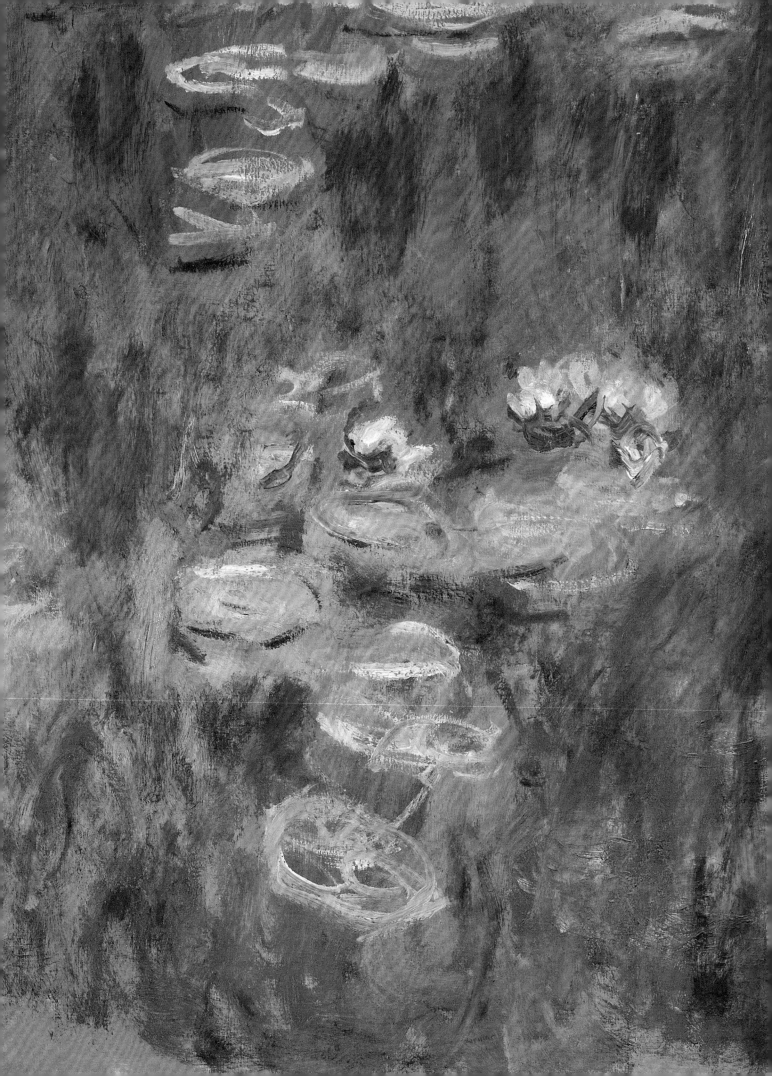

Monet's Water Lilies

Morning,1914-18,
oil on canvas,
197 x 1,270 cm.
(detail on following
double page)

Clouds, 1914-18,
oil on canvas,
197 x 1,271 cm.

and *Grandes Décorations, 1914–26*). Each marked a new stage in a revolutionary process that called into question the retinal vision of nature.

'An object for painting'

It all began in early 1893, when, at the end of the flower garden in the property he had moved into ten years earlier, the painter laid out a 'water garden' with a view to growing aquatic plants. He had the greatest difficulty obtaining authorisation from the prefect to have the waters of the River Epte diverted in order to allow this. The locals, too, were wary. But eventually, in July 1893, the prefect ruled in his favour. (The loss to art if he had refused hardly bears thinking about.) Monet claimed that his plans merely concerned 'An attractive feature to delight the eyes, and also an object for painting'. More precisely: a curved Japanese bridge over the pool on the western side, in a sinuous natural setting, soon to be surrounded by wisteria with a fragrance redolent of vanilla. Already, the following summer, Monet's friend Octave Mirbeau was in raptures over the 'marvellous water lilies and magical Japanese irises.' Still, over the next four years, Monet's art and his garden would develop separately. The artist was absorbed in his *Rouen Cathedral* series, his Norwegian landscapes and his series of *Mornings on the Seine*. As he later recalled, 'It took me some time to understand my water lilies [...] I grew them but did not think to paint them [...] You cannot become steeped in scenery overnight.'

But what of that French title, *Nymphéas*? This was the scientific name for the white water lily, an aquatic plant that fascinated many writers, not least the Romantics, for whom it had morbid and even maleficent associations. These connotations began to change when Mallarmé – the same Mallarmé who, returning from a visit to Giverny, wrote, 'One thing I am happy about is to be living in the age of Monet' – composed a long poem about the flower in 1885. But it was Monet who changed the way people referred to the water lily by establishing its scientific name, which speaks so vividly of the nymphs, those mythical daughters of springs and woods. In *Swann's Way* (1913), Proust mentions a dweller along the banks of the River Vivonne who has slowed down its flow so that the *nymphéas* form 'a veritable floating flower-bed' under which sparkles 'a kaleidoscope of silent, watchful and mobile contentment'. Although he had probably never been to Giverny, the writer, who, like Monet, was engaged in a colossal artistic quest, had, by one of those insights that came so often to him, understood that the *Water Lilies* represented much more than the culmination of an aesthetic vision.

Reinventing landscape

For, at the age of 53, Monet, who had been the leading figure of Impressionism, and who had already produced more than 1,300 paintings, wanted to go beyond the aesthetic of the moment, beyond those 'easy things' that were the notation and sensation

Monet's Water Lilies

Above:
Claude Monet in his
studio at Giverny in front
of a panel of the *Water
Lilies* for the Musée de
l'Orangerie, photo Henri
Manuel.

Georges Clemenceau and
Claude Monet at Giverny.

Page right:
Clouds, (detail of the
centre left panel),
1914-18, oil on canvas,
197 x 1271 cm.

of nature in a frame. He was going to reinvent landscape, without an easel, and with no horizon on the canvas. It would be a passionate, tormented quest, in which periods of exaltation alternated with spells of doubt and deep discouragement. He had to forget the appearance of reality and penetrate its depths in order to capture its complex structure and reveal the passing of time. Visual experience was now bound up with duration and would transcribe the movements of consciousness – one of the great themes of Monet's contemporary, Bergson.

From 1897 to his death, Monet would drive himself to exhaustion exploring the vision of the water, its reflections and depths, of the banks under their inextricable tangle of plant life. What was he expressing? The fluidity of the elements, the essential beauty amidst which man lives, a kind of cosmic infinity that the modern age, obsessed with tensions and disdainful of deeper emotions, tried to forget. In the course of those thirty years of work there would be many attempts, false starts and fresh explorations of abandoned paths. But the most astonishing aspect of all this was revealed in an article published by the journalist Maurice Guillemot in 1898. In the summer of 1897 Guillemot had visited Monet, who led him to his pond and there

spoke to him, of a 'decoration for which [Monet] has already begun to paint studies, large panels which he showed me afterward in his studio. Imagine a circular room in which the dado beneath the moulding is covered with [paintings] water, dotted with these plants to the very horizon, walls of a transparency alternately green and mauve, the calm and silence of the still waters reflecting the opened blossoms.' In 1897, then, Monet already had detailed ideas about what would find its finished form in the presentation at the Musée de l'Orangerie.

A challenge and an obsession

Around the edges of his pool, Monet found the world that he was looking for, that it would be his permanent challenge to convey. As the painter Riopelle would reflect in the 1970s: 'It's impossible to imagine paintings as huge, as measureless as these being made in front of a tiny little pond.'

Yes, but that pond was an ideal construction, a world of its own where the underwater interlacings of plants, the clouds of vapour reflected in the moiré surface of the water, declare the fleeting nuptials of water and sky and sketch out the ever-wider, ever-changing and ever-repeated circle where the painter took up position. The watery mirror

Monet's Water Lilies

Two Weeping Willows,
1914-18, oil on canvas,
197 x 1274 cm.

Morning no. 1,
1914-18, oil on canvas,
197 x 1700 cm.

Morning no. 2,
1914-18, oil on canvas,
197 x 1275 cm.

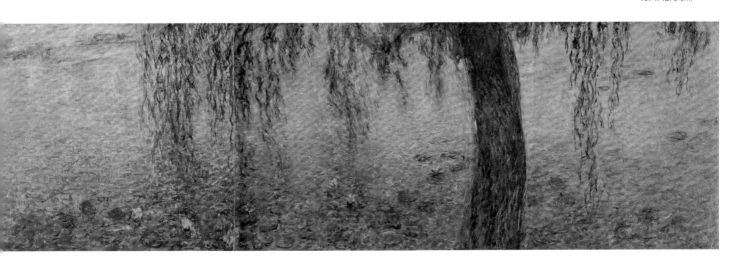

Monet's Water Lilies

was repeated ad infinitum and the painting itself never ceased, in a perpetual continuum like that of the universe itself. In 1908, Monet wrote to his friend Gustave Geffroy that 'these landscapes of water and reflections have become an obsession.' The previous year, Picasso painted *Les Demoiselles d'Avignon*, prompting his friend Braque to predict that, 'One day we shall find that he has hanged himself behind it'. But perhaps, the true 'madness' lay in Monet's landscapes of water, in that ultimate fluidity which broke irrevocably with the Western model of painting. One thing is certain: the path to abstraction passed through Giverny.

What was to be done with this painting that was beyond the understanding of the great majority of art lovers? Might it decorate a private home, as Whistler's work had done? In 1909 Monet told the critic Roger Marx that, 'For a moment, I was tempted to use this theme of the water lilies for the decoration of a drawing room: transposed along the walls, enveloping all the surfaces with its unity, it would have produced the illusion of an endless whole, of a wave without horizon or shore; there, following the restful example of these still waters, nerves strained by work would have relaxed and that room would have offered its occupant a haven of peaceful meditation amidst a flowering aquarium.' Marianne Alphant, the author of a remarkable biography of the painter, offers this perfect explanation of his final decision,

Setting Sun,
1914-18,
oil on canvas,
197 x 600 cm.

which was bound up with the very nature of the work: 'With the great *Water Lilies*, Monet was depending on no one but himself. The extraordinary prodigality of this painting placed it outside commercial circuits. Monet had understood the nature of the market more clearly than anyone else, and the time had come to free his last work. He decided to make a donation.'

A pantheistic poem against barbarism

On 12 November 1918, with the echo of the Armistice bells only just fading, the artist wrote to his dear friend Clemenceau: 'I am about to complete two decorative panels that I wish to seal with the day of Victory, and I write to ask if, through you, I may offer them to the State. It is not much, but it is the only way I have of taking part in the Victory. I wish these two panels to be placed in the Musée des Arts Décoratifs and I would be happy if you were the one to choose them.' It was a sublime offering, and supremely symbolic. In a country that lay in ruins, where a generation had been sacrificed in the mud of the trenches, an artist raised aloft the consoling power of civilisation. *The Water Lilies* against barbarism, what could be better? But there was more to come. For not only did Clemenceau patiently but persistently pressure his 'dear old Nutter' not to give up (the artist was discouraged by the cataract for which he had a late operation in 1923), he also encouraged him to produce

Monet's Water Lilies

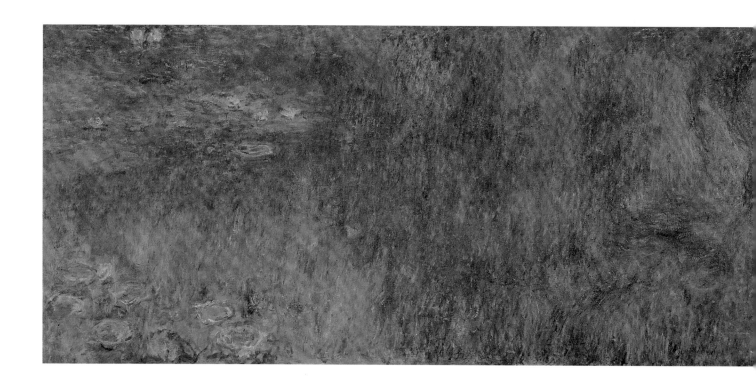

Reflections of Trees,
1914-18,
oil on canvas,
197 x 847 cm.

Green Reflections,
1914-18,
oil on canvas,
197 x 847 cm.

Monet's Water Lilies

more works. In the end, the ensemble delivered after Monet's death consisted of eight compositions comprising twenty-two panels: *Morning, Clouds, Green Reflections, Setting Sun, Reflections of Trees, Clear Morning with Weeping Willows, Morning with Weeping Willows and Two Weeping Willows*. The canvases were two metres high and, placed end to end, had a total length of 91 metres. Where to house them? The first idea was to build a round temple in the garden of the Hôtel de Biron, near the Musée Rodin. Then, in March 1921, Clemenceau made a visit to the Jeu de Paume and Orangerie, which had been requisitioned not long before by the Direction des Beaux-Arts. While the former struck him as too narrow, the second delighted him. 'I advise you to agree', he wrote to Monet. And so the deed of donation specifically made provision for two oval rooms in the Orangerie. The interior was entrusted to the architect Camille Lefèvre, who linked the two rooms in a double ellipse, presenting the *Water Lilies* in a handsome spatial and temporal unity, mounted directly on the wall and in natural lighting. The inauguration was held on 27 May 1927. The day before, Clemenceau came to meditate in front of – or *in* – this 'pantheistic poem' whose presence in the heart of Paris owed so much to his tenacity. Was it too late or too early for the Orangerie to become that long-awaited Musée Claude Monet? This was the period of the *retour à l'ordre* (return to order), when art was more classical than lyrical, more geometrical than emotional. The public did not understand the *Water Lilies* and kept away, and the Administration grew weary of this space that was always empty. It began using it for big temporary exhibitions and in 1960 the interior was radically changed to accommodate the Walter-Guillaume Collection, which had just been bequeathed to the State. *The Water Lilies* lost their natural lighting and became a sideshow in a confused, rambling interior. It was not until the spring of 2006 that the interior architecture planned by Monet would be restored. Those going to pay homage to his masterpiece might dwell on Péguy's words from 1913: 'Given that a very great painter painted twenty-seven and thirty-five times his famous water lilies, then when did he paint them best? [...] The logical impulse would be to say: the last time, because he knew most. But I say, on the contrary: the first, because he knew *least*.'

A Champion of Modern Art

Paul Guillaume was a key mover of Parisian cultural life in the first decades of the twentieth century. Advised by his friend Apollinaire, he established himself as a dealer representing De Chirico, Utrillo and Modigliani, and built up one of the finest European collections of modern art. BY PHILIPPE SAUNIER

André Derain,
Portrait of Madame Paul Guillaume in a Wide-Brimmed Hat
1828-29,
oil on canvas,
92 x 73 cm.

Amedeo Modigliani,
Portrait of Paul Guillaume,
Oil on cardboard mounted on cradled plywood, 105 x 75 cm.

When he died, the modern art dealer Paul Guillaume (1891–1934) left an enviable reputation as a great discoverer of talents and friend of artists. The world of 'living art' was in mourning, grieving for one of the most persuasive and fervent upholders of its cause. But amidst the chorus of praise, one or two discordant notes could also be heard: Guillaume, they said, was an astute businessman who owed his success and fortune to Guillaume Apollinaire; he had simply 'creamed off the dividends' of actions inspired to a great extent by the poet and friend of the Cubists, who had died young. These insinuations were not totally unfounded. By blotting the halo of one of its 'saints', they added a bit of complexity to the 'golden legend' of modern art. But is it so unusual for the course of a life to hinge on certain encounters, fortunate coincidences or, even, a little bit of calculation? How can one seriously level such a criticism at a man who made no secret of his enormous debt to the author of *Alcools*? He was lucky? Sure, but he had the intelligence and the talent to

make something of it and, above all, never to give up.

Following the 'Blessed Enchanter'

Paul Guillaume was not even twenty when he started spending time with the lively and richly promising Bohemian crowd that gravitated around Place Ravignan and the Bateau-Lavoir. Living on Place Pigalle, right by Montmartre, Guillaume 'was present at the conversations between Apollinaire, Picasso and Braque at the Café Cyrano in 1910. No one knew who he was. He kept his own counsel and listened to what was being said at the painters' table', recalled the wife of the Cubist painter Marcoussis. Guillaume was under the spell of the brightest star in France's poetic firmament, Guillaume Apollinaire, nicknamed 'the Galvanising Enchanter' by Gonzague-Frick (in an allusion to the poet's *L'Enchanteur pourrissant*). But Guillaume would not have been so fascinated had he not been gifted with a real sensibility and deep love of art. Already, in those days, with his limited means, he was

Paul Guillaume in his gallery at 6 Rue de Miromesnil, Paris, circa 1914.

Page right:
Guillaume Apollinaire and Adolphe Basler in Paul Guillaume's flat/gallery, 16 Avenue de Villiers, circa 1916.

Paul Guillaume and Amedeo Modigliani in Nice, circa 1918.

buying works by Picasso from the dealers Sagot and Berthe Weil. How he went from being Apollinaire's discreet but attentive table companion to his friend, we cannot say. Were they introduced by a mutual acquaintance? Or did Apollinaire himself take him under his wing when he saw the African sculptures that the young man exhibited in the window of a garage where he was working? In any case, the relationship confirmed what had been Guillaume's more or less confused sense of his vocation: he would devote himself to dealing in the modern art that he so ardently supported. Guillaume had no special claim to fame, but he had grasped the modern beauty of African idols. That was enough for Apollinaire to help him make a start in the business of avant-garde art. Guillaume was taken on by gallery owner André Groult, whose wife was a close friend of none other than Marie Laurencin, the poet's mistress.

Backed by the prestige of Apollinaire, Guillaume put all his youthful passion into the bold enterprise of opening his own gallery. Located on Rue Miromesnil, this was inaugurated in February 1914, and

Guillaume boldly stated that it would be devoted 'to the best contemporary artists'. Its main holdings were works by Picabia and De Chirico – still relative unknowns – along with African sculptures, for which he soon established himself as the specialist. The relation with Apollinaire grew closer, and the two men were soon engaged in a real professional collaboration. Apollinaire ensured press coverage of the gallery's opening and prefaced the catalogue for Guillaume's first show, which featured the two young Russian painters Goncharova and Larionov.

A masterstroke

The outbreak of war in August 1914 threatened the fledgling gallery. Rejected by the army for health reasons, Guillaume stayed in Paris but the slump in business forced him to close. In 1916, he set up again in a modest flat on Rue de Villiers. His unshakeable confidence soon overcame any momentary discouragement. He was daring and spunky, ready to react. Paris had lost most of its major dealers and artistic life was sluggish. Here, he sensed, was an opportunity: he would become the 'Plenipotentiary of modern art'. Kahnweiler, the leading dealer of Cubist art, a German, left Paris for Switzerland. Guillaume thought he might take his place and mentioned this to Apollinaire, who had volunteered for the front. Before calling on Derain, Picasso, Braque or Laurencin, he asked his mentor about prices. Alas, they were no longer unknowns. The prospect of signing affordable contracts with them seemed increasingly remote.

Instead, the young man would have to pin his hopes on promising but more affordable painters. Here he played his hand brilliantly, choosing three remarkable but relatively little-known painters: the Italian De Chirico (whom he met through Apollinaire), Utrillo ('Go for him', prompted the poet) and Modigliani. For two years, he managed to be Modigliani's sole buyer, and provider of regular income. When Modigliani's health forced him to give up sculpture, Guillaume encouraged him to devote himself to painting and was ready to pay the rent on a studio in Montmartre. He offered De Chirico a contract whereby he would be paid (a mere) 120 francs for six paintings a month. And, finally, he bought up dozens of paintings by Utrillo, either from the artist himself, or from Marie Visier, whose cabaret owned what he considered the painter's 'finest works'. Even so, he was taking a risk. There was no guarantee that prices for these 'youngsters' would soar. Sure of their talent,

Guillaume built up stocks of their works, wagering on a brilliant future. He worked tirelessly to exhibit and sell them, while pursuing a more lucrative parallel activity as an antiques dealer. Classical objects sold more easily to a clientele seeking reassurance in uncertain times.

The 'Bridge'

Guillaume's strategy during the slump of the war years involved much more than stocking up and waiting for better days. Success could only be ensured by the intensive and dynamic promotion of the gallery, of its painters and African sculptures. To become a major player in the modern art trade, he needed to make a name for himself and acquire a reputation as a friend to artists, and thus gain their trust. A series of events over the next four years would establish the gallery at the heart of the avant-garde.

In 1916 he put on an exhibition of work by Derain, with the hope of winning over the painter and becoming his dealer. He did not achieve this until 1923, but in the meantime he at least got people talking about him. In April 1917 he published an album with photographs of some of the finest African pieces, many of them his own. He was also careful to place them in his friends' exhibitions. At the end of 1917, with signs of an economic upturn, Guillaume opened a gallery on Rue du Faubourg Saint-Honoré.

Paul Guillaume
in his gallery at
59 Rue La Boétie, Paris,
after 1922.

Page right:
Paul Guillaume's office
at his home on Avenue
du Bois (now Avenue
Foch), between
1930 and 1933.

Here, he began to attract a broader public. 'It was a fine private view, with poets, painters, actors, collectors and people from society and finance, the whole of Modernist Paris, twisting and craning to see the canvases on the walls', noted one observer. Apollinaire inaugurated the gallery with a *causerie* (there was also a poetry reading and a recital of Satie piano music), and on 18 February it put on a much-noted exhibition of works by Matisse and Picasso. In February 1918 Guillaume launched his own journal, *Les Arts à Paris*, then exhibited works by De Chirico on the stage of the Vieux-Colombier theater and organised *fêtes nègres*: he was a genuine cultural player. '*Novo pilota*' was the nickname coined by Modigliani for this young man who had begun to drive the world of modern art with the assurance of an accomplished rally racer, mixing insouciant assurance and a keen sense of risk.

Apollinaire was a superb co-pilot. In 1915 he had urged his protégé to look after the gallery: 'I'll be needing it after the war'. The poet saw it as a platform for a leading role in cultural life. For him, the gallery was a tool for uniting the development of literature and the visual arts, providing they were modern. Never in the front line, he pulled strings and developed his influence. As Guillaume later noted: 'His magic charisma brought on the blossoming of many an unwitting talent. […] It would be impossible to mention all the artists to whom he was the bright sun, and who came alive when they were exposed to his astonishing imagination.' As for Guillaume, he proved a magnificent intermediary. No wonder the poet called him 'the Bridge'.

Private passion and public cause: an extraordinary collection

After the poet's death at the end of 1918, Guillaume's activity waned slightly. As the art market took off, he reaped the fruit of his multifarious activities. In the early 1920s he met the American billionaire Alfred Barnes and became his prime purveyor of modern paintings, which brought him huge profits. He moved his gallery to the very plush Rue La Boétie and consolidated the collection he began building at the start of his career, giving it a real creative dimension: he fine-tuned the hanging, brought out echoes between paintings, and savoured the contrasts between 'other' art (African and Khmer sculptures) and works by Derain, Matisse, Picasso, Soutine, Utrillo, Goerg and Fautrier. A welcoming host to the visitors who came from all over the world to see his collection, in 1927 he spoke of opening a 'museum hotel' (the influence of the Barnes Foundation in Philadelphia, no doubt) and donating it to the State. In doing so, he would be fulfilling the wishes of his mentor. In 1914, Apollinaire had called for 'the creation of a truly modern museum'. It was he said, 'unacceptable that a country such as France […] should, to those wishing to see this artistic prosperity for themselves, have nothing more to show than the paintings at the Luxembourg, two thirds of which are by artists who, while certainly distinguished, have played no role in the history of art.'

In 1929, Guillaume's collection was shown at the Bernheim gallery. It was one of the most important collections of modern art in Europe, both in quantity and in quality. The politicians and senior civil servants who attended the inauguration put the seal of official recognition on Guillaume's action as champion of the finest art of the day. The collection did not exist solely for the pleasure of its owner: it was an act of witness, a tool and an expression of his struggle that all could see. 'Paul Guillaume made it the instrument of his action. Putting it together, he forged the tool that brought about the triumph of his ideas. He rendered a magnificent service to the painters he loved by bringing together works of which they were proud, by forming a whole that had a meaning, a direction', observed the critic André Warnod. Weary of the art business – 'at thirty-five, I felt my fire had died,' he told the critic Tériade – Guillaume now sought to go down in posterity while working in the public interest. However, the financial difficulties resulting from the collapse of the

1930s, and the collector's own reluctance to part with his creation, delayed the process. Paul considered making a bequest to the Louvre, but his death at the age of forty-four left his ambitious project hanging.

After various ups and downs, Domenica, his widow, who in 1941 married the architect and businessman Jean Walter, eventually sold the collection to the State, thereby doing justice to a man of whom Tériade wrote in 1927, that, 'He deserves to figure among those few pioneers or explorers of modern painting whose role went beyond acquiring stocks of established, guaranteed and unquestionable names. He was a fighter, one of those who supported the movement in its budding days, in its period of uncertainty, boldly fighting the battle of new ideas with his writings, his tireless activity and his knowledge.'∎

Selections from the

Above:
Nude amid Landscape,
1883, oil on canvas,
65 x 54 cm.

Bather with Long Hair,
circa 1895, oil on canvas,
82 x 65 cm.

Right:
*Reclining Nude
(Gabrielle),*
1906-1907, oil on
canvas, 67 x 160 cm.

Walter-Guillaume Collection

Pierre-Auguste Renoir

A friend of Monet and Sisley, in 1874 Pierre-Auguste Renoir (1841–1919) took part in what has since come to be known as the first Impressionist exhibition, in the studio of the photographer Nadar. However, it was not until the 1880s that he really found the style that expressed his deeper self. A journey to Italy in October 1881 was among the events that led him to turn his back on Impressionism and to rediscover the authority of form, something that his fellows were tending to neglect in their concern with light. The human figure, and in particular the female nude (*Bather with Long Hair*), became his favourite subject. He expressed his love of full forms in big, robust and exuberant nudes that, especially in his maturity, expressed his hedonism (*Reclining Nude [Gabrielle]*). As portrayed by Renoir, a nude woman is a purely animal being. Whether seen against foamy water or foliage, she is like a hyper-natural fruit of the flesh that has grown to ripeness amidst an infinitely pagan and ingenuous Nature.

Pierre-Auguste Renoir

Although rejected by the new avant-garde after 1910 – as Picasso would recall, 'We were 25, Renoir was triumphant, we had to do something different' –, the 'Master of Cagnes' (he moved to this town on the Mediterranean coast in 1900) was back in favour less than ten years later. People had grown weary of the austere and intellectual grammar of Cubism. Renoir's great nudes, with their hypertrophied thighs and opulent breasts, offered the fertile and generous contours of a pacified modernism, and the welcome sense of a living presence in art. It was Renoir's vision of womanhood, 'heavy with her fecundity, tied to the earth by her powerful, soft limbs' (Jean Labasque) that gave birth to Picasso's *Bathers* (1921).

PHILIPPE SAUNIER

Apples and Pears,
1890-1895,
oil on canvas,
32 x 41 cm.

Strawberries,
1915-1917,
oil on canvas,
28 x 46 cm.

Page right:
Blonde Girl with Rose,
circa 1920,
oil on canvas,
65 x 53 cm.

Above:
Young Girls at the Piano,
circa 1892,
oil on canvas,
116 x 81 cm.

Right:
Gabrielle and Jean,
1895-1896,
oil on canvas,
65 x 54 cm.

Left:
*Claude Renoir in Clown
Costume*, 1909,
oil on canvas,
120 x 77 cm.

Page left:
Portrait of the Artist's Son,
circa 1881-1882,
oil on canvas,
35 x 38 cm.

Above:
*Portrait of
Madame Cézanne,*
circa 1890,
oil on canvas,
81 x 65 cm.

Paul
Cézanne

In a letter written from the front in April 1915, Apollinaire
advised Paul Guillaume to buy 'inexpensive paintings:
Rousseau, Picasso, Laurencin, Bonnard, Cézanne, etc.'
Cézanne (1839–1906) was brought to wider art world
attention by the dealer Ambroise Vollard, starting in 1895,
and it was from Vollard that Guillaume bought several of his
works for his own collection, including two portraits of
Madame Cézanne. However most of the paintings that
constitute today's Walter-Guillaume Collection were bought
by Guillaume's widow, Domenica, in the 1950s. A number of
her choices were symbolic: she bought pieces similar to
those acquired but not kept by her husband. Thus *Trees
and Houses* can be compared to the painting of the same
title at the Metropolitan Museum, New York, and *The Boat
and Bathers* can be linked to the *Four Bathers* at the
Barnes Foundation in Merion.

Paul Cézanne

At the sale of the Ernest Cognacq Collection in 1952, Domenica (now remarried, to Jean Walter) caused a sensation by paying what, in those days, was the colossal price of 33 million francs for *Apples and Biscuits*. The auctioneer, Maurice Rheims, saw this as the first phase in the vertiginous rise in art market prices that took place during these years. He added that the purchase was an excellent investment for Domenica, for it cast a flattering light on her collection. Certainly, it is thanks to Domenica Walter's judicious 'investments' that the Musée de l'Orangerie is able to boast a comprehensive ensemble of works by the French master, including some uncontested masterpieces. MARIE-LAURE CROSNIER LECONTE

Page left:
Apples and Biscuits,
circa 1880,
oil on canvas,
46 x 55 cm.

Above:
Straw-trimmed Vase,
Sugar Bowl and Apples,
1890-1893,
oil on canvas,
36 x 46 cm.

Paul Cézanne

*In the Park
at Château Noir,*
1898, oil on canvas,
92 x 73 cm.

Page right:
Boats and Bathers
(general view and detail),
circa 1888, oil on canvas,
30 x 1.25 cm.

Amedeo
Modigliani

The Italian painter and sculptor Amedeo Modigliani came to Paris in 1906. In the second decade of the century, his position in Parisian artistic life was fairly similar to that of Marie Laurencin. Combining elements of the 'fin-de-siècle' aesthetic with new developments in modern art (the rough brushstrokes in *Woman with Velvet Ribbon*, the almost textual quotation of Cézanne's proto-Cubist *Smoker* in *The Young Apprentice*), he painted singular heroines who, like Laurencin's, were subtly reminiscent of the creatures painted by Burne-Jones and his fellow Pre-Raphaelite. 'The hieratic quality of the stylisation places Modigliani's work in the sphere of symbolic realities: he disembodies his figures, making them into waking dreamers; he gives them [...] the disenchanted gaze of those whose dream has met with the world as it really is' (Roger Brielle, 1933).

It was inevitable that Paul Guillaume would be drawn to Modigliani, whose direct carving produced sculptures that were similar to African fetishes in their stylistic simplification and often crude appearance. During the two years when he acted as his exclusive agent (1915–16), Guillaume brought the artist relative financial security (before then, Modigliani used to sell his drawings for the ridiculously low price of fifty centimes or a franc): 'He was shy, distinguished, one of life's aristocrats, but his clothes hardly inspired confidence and if by any chance someone did spare him a little money, they generally pestered him a bit, too. I do hope that I will not be greatly contradicted if I say that, from the moment when I knew him this sad situation came to an end', recalled Guillaume in 1920, shortly after his protégé's death.

PH. S.

Woman with Velvet Neckband,
circa 1915,
oil on canvas mounted on cardboard,
54 x 45.5 cm.

Page right:
The Young Apprentice,
1918-19,
oil on canvas,
100 x 65 cm.

Below:
Old Man Juniet's Trap,
1908, oil on canvas,
97 x 129 cm.

Page right:
Child with Doll,
1904-1905, oil on
canvas, 67 x 52 cm.

The Wedding Party,
circa 1905, oil on canvas,
163 x 114 cm.

Henri
Rousseau

Henri Rousseau was known as 'Le Douanier' because of the job he held at the customs office in Paris after the 1870 Franco-Prussian war. Discovered by Alfred Jarry, this self-taught artist only acquired a certain fame late in his life, when, after 1900, artists looking to make a final break with the formulae and allegiance to reality of late Impressionism turned towards Rousseau and his genius for simplification. Adolphe Basler, a friend of Apollinaire and Paul Guillaume, analysed this belated 'cult' as follows: 'Following his nature, the art of this divine primitive, in its very chasteness, stands apart from all the slovenliness and all the tricks of the trade, from all cerebral or sensual perversities'. Apollinaire's enthusiasm for 'Le Douanier' began in 1907, and he helped win over many artists, among them Robert Delaunay, Picasso and Serge Férat, who would later sell *The Wedding Party* to Paul Guillaume. The (relative) naivety and element of awkwardness (approximate perspectives, awkward figures) in Rousseau's paintings introduced a poetic element into the representation of reality. His seraphic skies, his stylised trees and plants and his meadows, reminiscent of old high-warp tapestries (*Child with Doll*) made him a primitive of modern art. 'Rousseau is the return of the Angel to art' (Florent Fels, 1931). Not only did he freely express his imagination (his jungles and virgin forests seem to have been taken straight out of the painter's dreams), but he introduced a sense of the monumental that contrasted with the disintegration of the Impressionist touch. Paul Guillaume was one of the main collectors of Rousseau's paintings, which Apollinaire had been urging him to buy — 'at a good price', naturally — as of 1915.

Ph. S.

Marie Laurencin

In around the year 1910, Marie Laurencin was one of the foremost figures in the world of new art. While her diaphanous young girls may have lost some of their magic over the years, when she started out they had an undeniably modern feel. In 1907, Laurencin entered the circle of artists and poets that had formed around Picasso and Apollinaire (with whom she had a passionate affair). Initially influenced by the chromatic boldness and simplifications of Fauvism, the 'Fauvette' then became 'Notre-Dame du Cubisme': 'The little I have learnt was taught me by those I call the great painters: Matisse, Derain, Picasso, Braque', she would later say.

But what really made Laurencin original was the intense and very personal poetry of her work, its contrasting mix of strangeness and enigma with an elegance and refinement that never undermines its authenticity. The profound singularity of her heroines reflects Laurencin's own solitary status among her fellow artists. 'Her figures can do nothing for us, and we can do nothing for them', observed Jean Cocteau. Paul Guillaume met Laurencin through Apollinaire in 1911 or 1912. By then she was already a recognised artist, under contract with Paul Rosenberg. But while not her official dealer, Guillaume bought and sold large numbers of her works. Laurencin became a figure in Parisian society and, was a friend of Guillaume and his wife Domenica, whose portrait she painted in the 1920s.   PH. S.

Les Biches,
1923, oil on canvas,
73 x 92 cm.

Page right:
*Portrait of
Mademoiselle Chanel,*
1924, oil on canvas,
92 x 73 cm.

Page left:
The Adolescents,
1906, oil on canvas,
157 x 117 cm.

Right:
The Embrace,
1903, pastel,
98 x 57 cm.

Pablo Picasso

It was in 1912 that Paul Guillaume first made contact with Picasso (1881–1973), because of their shared passion for African art: 'I have heard from Monsieur Apollinaire that you are interested in my Negro statues.' In 1915, with Kahnweiler, Picasso's official dealer since 1907, forced to leave France, Guillaume hoped to attract the artist to his own gallery, but he was beaten to it by the Rosenberg brothers, who had greater financial clout than he did. And so the young gallerist had to make do with Picassos from indirect sources. However, he never lost his interest in the painter and in early 1918 he took up a suggestion of Apollinaire's and organised an exhibition of both Picasso and Matisse. However, it was hastily prepared and neither painter attended the opening. Worse, they were angered at the brash publicity around their name in time of war (Gaumont produced a newsreel on the exhibition). Apparently, though, they did not bear Guillaume a grudge, for in December that same year he put on a new exhibition featuring some forty of their works. He later bought a large number of Picassos for his private collection. In 1926, for example, dazzled by what he had seen at the Barnes Foundation in Philadelphia, and with the art market reaching new peaks, he was able to buy *Woman in White* for what, at the time, was a record price for Picasso. More open than Dr Barnes was to the variety of the painter's work, Guillaume bought some of the Cubist paintings, but seemed less interested by the new direction taken in 1925. Sadly, Domenica was less receptive to the great genius of the century and sold some essential pieces. M.-L. C. L.

Pablo Picasso

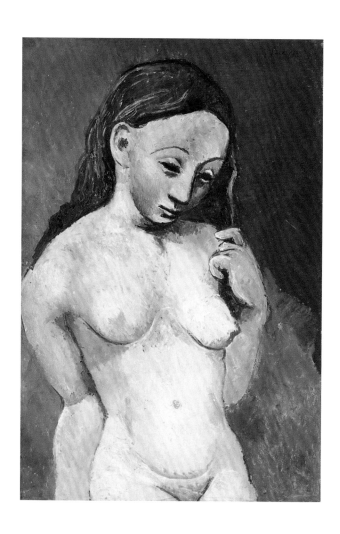

Right:
Nude on Red Background,
circa 1905-1906,
oil on canvas,
81 x 54 cm.

Below:
Woman with Tambourine,
1925, oil on canvas,
97 x 130 cm.

Page right:
Large Bather,
1921, oil on canvas,
182 x 101.5 cm.

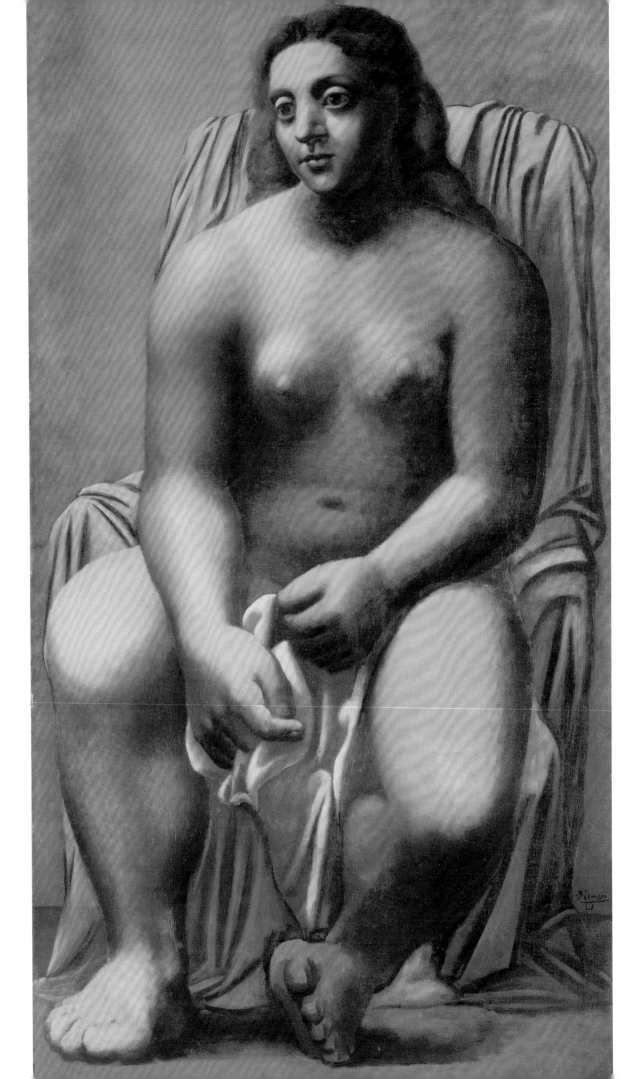

Henri Matisse

Unlike Picasso, Henri Matisse (1869–1954) did not belong to Apollinaire's circle. As Marguerite, Matisse's daughter, would later recall, when Guillaume approached the artist in 1916 he employed a subterfuge that he used often in those early days and passed himself off as Max Jacob's secretary. Matisse had an exclusive contract with Bernheim-Jeune, but in 1917 he gained the right to keep half his work, and his name now began to appear in the advertisements that Guillaume published in the press. However, at Guillaume's famous joint show by the two 'Greats' of modern painting, Matisse and Picasso, organised in January 1918, most of the Matisses came from the Bernheim gallery's reserves. The exhibition also featured *The Three Sisters*, a work that was to become one of the major holdings of the Barnes Foundation. Matisse now became, almost unwittingly, one of the pillars of the gallery. His relations with Guillaume were erratic. Matisse spent most of his time in Nice, where Guillaume paid him several visits. He reproached the artist for not telling him what he

Henri Matisse

Left:
Odalisque in Red Trousers,
1921. oil on canvas,
50 x 61 cm.
© Estate of H. Matisse.

Above:
Blue Odalisque
or *The White Slave*,
1921-1922, oil on canvas,
82 x 54 cm.
© Estate of H. Matisse..

had to sell, but the truth was that Matisse found the dealer's precious, emphatic manner hard to take. And yet in 1926 Guillaume persuaded him to part with two masterpieces, *Bathers by the River* and *The Piano Lesson*, which he boldly exhibited in his gallery, accompanied only by *Bouquet of Flowers*, also by Matisse. Almost exactly at this time, at the Pellerin sale, he bought the canvas that would come to be called *The Three Sisters*. It is interesting to note that he had just come back from Merion, and that *The Piano Lesson* and *The Three Sisters* were bought with the Barnes Collection in mind. Of the 126 works from Guillaume's personal collection shown at Bernheim-Jeune in 1929, 19 were by Matisse. Sadly, however, these, along with the Picassos, were the main victims of the sales by the dealer's widow after 1934. These left only *The Three Sisters* and the canvases from the Nice period (1917–1929).   M.-L. C. L.

André Derain

André Derain is the artist who features most prominently in the Walter-Guillaume Collection, even though the 28 canvases here cover only ten years of his career, the period of the so-called 'retour à l'ordre', when Derain followed the classical masters and produced highly structured, realistic works, mainly nudes and still lifes.

During the war, when Derain was at the front and Kahnweiler out of France, Alice, Derain's wife, with the help of Apollinaire, organised the first exhibition of her husband's work in Guillaume's flat on Avenue de Villiers. Although press coverage was modest, the thirty-odd paintings sold well and set the young dealer on the path to prosperity.

At the end of the war, Kahnweiler went about re-establishing his business, and resuming relations with his painters. But Guillaume tirelessly cultivated Derain and became his exclusive dealer in 1923.

Above:
The Painter's Niece,
circa 1931. oil on canvas,
171 x 77 cm.

Right:
*Black Man with
Mandolin,*
circa 1930, oil on canvas,
92 x 73 cm.

Page right:
Harlequin and Pierrot,
1924, oil on canvas,
175 x 175 cm.

André Derain

Above:
The Kitchen Table,
circa 1922,
oil on canvas,
119 x 119 cm.

Page left:
Southern Landscape,
1932-1933,
oil on canvas,
65 x 54 cm.

Their relationship became almost symbiotic, a strange tandem of dominant and dominated, as described somewhat suggestively by Alberto Savinio in his memoirs: Derain, always needing money, and constantly supported by his new dealer, while, 'more than his painterly genius' it was 'Derain's tall frame, his nonchalance as a peaceful giant that acted on Paul Guillaume.'

Harlequin and Pierrot, the large-format painting that Guillaume commissioned from the painter, is an artistic testimony to their relation, in which the face of the Pierrot figure is his portrait. But in spite of the sometimes brutal way Derain had of exploiting his power of attraction over his dealer, it is not clear which of the two was the more dependent. Guillaume's sudden death in 1934 left Derain at a loss. He moved to Chambourcy and put an end to all commercial commitments.   M.-L. C. L.

André Derain

Le Beau Modèle,
1923, oil on canvas,
115 x 90 cm.

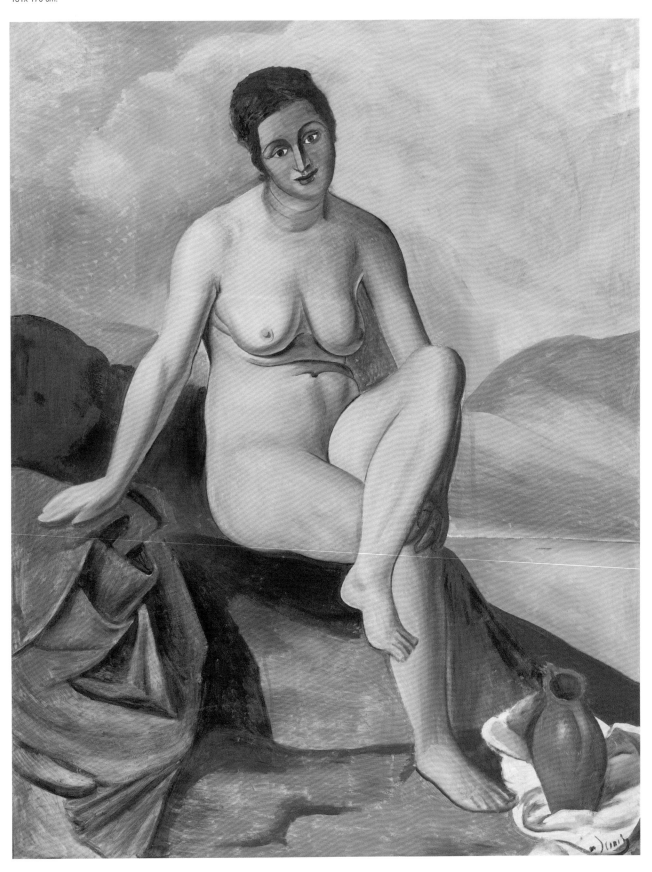

Maurice Utrillo

Born into the same generation as Picasso, Laurencin and Modigliani, Maurice Utrillo (1883–1955) never belonged to any established artistic group. A prickly, sensitive individual, he became an alcoholic in his teens and was prone to fits of violence. His mother, Susan Valadon, was a painter, but from her he learnt little more than the rudiments and he was basically self-taught. Utrillo started painting in 1903, at first in Pierrefitte and then in Montmagny. His work was dominated by a number of recurring motifs that he treated with his own distinctive vigour, following his instinct as he applied thick layers of paint. His exploration of the expressive qualities of impasto culminated in the works of his 'white period' (1910-1914). Behind these peeling, seedy exteriors, the painter was pursuing the very ambitious goal of capturing the material nature of reality: 'I had got it into my head that only plaster, real plaster, would give me marvellous results, true things on my cardboard, grass, the leaves of trees.' It is hard not see this vehement art, and the singularly gestural painting that went into it (paint applied as if by a mason, kneaded, scraped and scratched) as the manifestation of suffering, of torment. Beyond the picturesque celebration of Montmartre to which his art is all too often reduced, Utrillo can be linked to the finest European expressionists, notably Fautrier (the *Hostages* series), whom Paul Guillaume also supported.   PH. S.

Above:
Big Cathedral
or *Orléans Cathedral,*
1909 or 1913,
oil on cardboard,
73 x 54 cm.

Right:
Berlioz's House,
13 September 1914,
oil on panel,
74 x 104 cm.

Page right:
La Butte Pinson,
between 1905 and 1908,
oil on cardboard,
48 x 37 cm.

Chaïm
Soutine

The sudden rise to fame of Chaïm Soutine (1893–1943) was described by Paul Guillaume in the January 1923 issue of his journal *Les Arts à Paris*: 'One day in January 1923 when I went to look at a Modigliani painting in someone's studio, I spotted a work in a corner that greatly excited me. It was a Soutine, and it represented a pastry cook – an extraordinary pastry cook: fascinating, real, earthy, cursed with a huge, superb ear, unexpected and just right: a masterpiece. I bought it. Dr Barnes saw it at my place. "But it's a peach", he exclaimed. The spontaneous pleasure he felt on seeing that canvas would be the cause of Soutine's sudden fortune.' The artist came to Paris from his native Lithuania in 1913 and, through his friend Modigliani, met

Above:
The Village,
1923-1924,
oil on canvas,
75 x 93 cm.

Page right:
The Choirboy,
1928, oil on canvas,
69 x 49 cm.

Chaïm Soutine

the dealer Léopold Zborowski in 1917, although it was only the year
after that the latter, who was wary of his unstable character, signed
him up. As for Guillaume, it would seem that that the only Soutine he
ever had at his gallery was *The Little Pastry Cook*, as mentioned in
the story Indeed, when Guillaume took Barnes to Zborowksi's gallery
the American bought up all Soutine's recent works, thereby triggering
the interest of other dealers. Guillaume, too, followed the trend and
bought at least two other works for himself, *The Little Pastry Cook
of Cagnes,* and the work now exhibited at the Musée de l'Orangerie,
The Room-Service Waiter. In fact, he built up the biggest collection
of Soutine's works in Europe.

Soutine's use of pure colours, dripped or slashed across the canvas,
his fascination with red and white, and, above all, the impulsive
violence of his gesture, all anticipate the gestural painting
of the American Abstract Expressionists, and in particular Willem
De Kooning and Jackson Pollock.   M.-L. C. L.

Above:
*The Rabbit and
the Iron Dish,*
1923-1924,
oil on canvas,
73 x 36 cm.

Facing:
The Table,
circa 1919, oil on canvas,
81 x 100 cm.

Page right:
*Side of Beef and
Calf's Head,*
1925, oil on canvas,
92 x 73 cm.

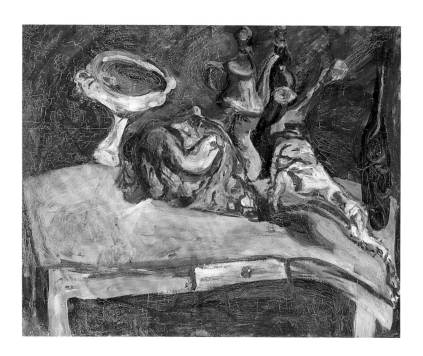

Visitor Information

Musée de l'Orangerie
Jardin des Tuileries
75001 Paris
Tel: +33 (0)1 44 77 80 07
musee.orangerie@culture.gouv.fr

Opening hours
Open daily except Tuesdays,
1 May and 25 December.
• Individual visitors:
12:30–19:00 (Friday: 21:00).
• Groups: 9:00–12:30,
by written reservation,
fax: +33 (0)1 44 77 81 12. Free
on the first Sunday of each
month.

Access
Métro: Concorde

Bus: 24, 42, 52, 72, 73, 84, 94
(stop: Concorde)
Parking: Jardin des Tuileries
and Carrousel (access via Quai
des Tuileries or Rue de
Rivoli), Rue du Mont-Thabor,
Rue des Pyramides.

Events
• Temporary exhibitions are
presented on the lower ground
floor.
• The film room (lower ground
floor) presents continuous
screenings of documentary
films related to the permanent
collections and temporary shows.
• Talks about the exhibitions
are given on Fridays at 19:00

(duration: 1 h).
• Guided tours are available for
the permanent collections and
temporary exhibitions, for all
publics. Details are available
from the information desk.

Services
• Audio guide: commentaries
on selected works in French,
English, German, Spanish,
Italian, Japanese and Chinese.
• Wheelchair access
(wheelchairs available).
• Bookshop/boutique:
9:00–18:30 (Friday: 20:30).